FEARLESS BUSINESS BLUEPRINT

How To Build a Thriving, Sustainable and Profitable Business

ROBIN WAITE

First Published in Great Britain 2025 by Robin M Waite

Paperback ISBN 978-1-0682164-0-4

Robin Waite Limited

The Jollies, Selsley West, Stroud, Gloucestershire GL5 5LJ

www.robinwaite.com

Design: Sapna Pieroux

www.innervisions-id.com

About your authors

Robin Waite is the Founder of Fearless Business, regular speaker at various business events and bestselling author of several books, including *Online Business Startup*, *Marketing Machine* and the recent popular release *Take Your Shot.*

From 2004 to 2016 Robin led a successful marketing agency serving over 250 clients, delivering workshops and masterclasses that helped over 1,000 business owners improve their marketing, product architecture, pricing, websites and digital advertising.

Robin now heads up Fearless Business, a business coaching accelerator for Coaches, Consultants and Freelancers, helping them to productise their offer, increase their prices and confidently sell more.

Behind the scenes, Robin is a husband and father to two young girls, a surfer and Sunday warrior (road cyclist). He hates going up the hills but is well known at his local cycling club for descending at speeds more than 50mph down said hills.

Robin holds a Guinness World Record for participating in the largest ever speed networking event, has raised over £5,000 for a local Children's charity in the last four years and has a goal to help remove 100kg of plastic from the World's Oceans within the next twelve months via another charity he supports, 4Ocean.

www.robinwaite.com and **www.fearless.biz**

Sapna Pieroux is the brains behind the Fearless and Robin's own brand, a multi-award-winning personal and business brand consultant, designer, bestselling author of *Let's Get Visible!* (Business Book Awards winner), motivational and expert speaker.

After 20+ years in media (emap, The Telegraph, Chrysalis, Mirror Group, O2) with clients such as Mercedes, L'Oréal and PlayStation, Sapna's taken that big-brand know-how to build SME and entrepreneurial businesses.

"Easily one of the leading brand experts in the world" according to Robin and called 'SuperSaps' by her clients, Sapna's VISION Process® is so powerful, she can rebrand a business in a day and build standout personal brands. Really, her ultimate superpower is helping the world see *yours*.

Sapna has been a brand partner to Rethink Press, a brand mentor for a business accelerator, a business mentor for the University of West London and has guest lectured at Hult International Business School, Brunel University and the University of Northumbria.

She is married Andy, mum to two footy-mad boys and lives in London. She loves her Peloton, galleries and karaoke (so much so, that she started 'The NotWorkers' - networking for business owners with more joy, fun and real connection - as an excuse to go more often!). Passionate about all kinds of transformation, Sapna is also a qualified interior designer and a volunteer stylist for charity Smart Works, helping women into work.

www.innervisions-id.com
Ready to rebrand?: www.letsgetvisiblequiz.scoreapp.com

Confession time...

In October 2018, I was driving out to Cheltenham to see a client, when suddenly I had several epiphanies in one short 45-minute journey.

I don't recall which audiobook I was listening to at the time, but it was sheeting with rain and traffic had ground to a halt. I remember feeling tired, ever so tired, I was constantly running late for consultations and appointments with clients. Trying to be everywhere.

Yet every speaking engagement created even more work...normally a good thing, right? But I was already over capacity for clients, with over 20 one-to-one clients already engaged.

I would come home after my sessions and spend the evening writing up notes or frantically pulling together a presentation for a talk I was giving the next morning.

My amazing wife, Charlotte, would often look at me with sympathy in the evenings when I finally had time to give her my attention, and often tell me, "*Slow down, Robin, you're going to burn yourself out!*" And she was right.

Can you imagine; the busy business coach with little time for his family, rushing around hither and thither, trying to make a dent in the world but checking his bank balance daily thinking, *"Where's all the money, the reward, for all this hard work?"*

And yes...there were good days.

Paid speaking engagements or the occasional lucrative consulting gig for a day or two.

I put my prices up and launched a few online events. But...it made things worse.

That just attracted a whole new breed of clients with different problems.

I finally realised: I needed to fire some clients.

This was so demoralising. I loved working with all of my clients, my whole core values to this point had been based around impact. How could I be making an impact if I was helping FEWER business owners? Every week I let one or two clients go (swap that out for "let them down").

When I got to twelve clients, balance was restored, things felt manageable, time slowed down. I got to see my family more.

However my bank balance was taking a beating. Surely, I, a respected business coach, should be able to have fewer clients and make more money. *"Come on Robin!"* I used to say to myself, *"You've been in business for 15 years, your whole thing is about problem solving, why can't you figure this out?"* I did some simple maths.

The answer was simple, the twelve clients would need to be producing the same income as the 20+ clients I'd had previously.

So I spoke to them, they all agreed fee increases, after all I'd added value to their businesses. This capacity-based pricing approach saved my practice.

There was an unexpected benefit; my clients started asking questions about their own prices.

Russ, for example, wanted to know how he could have fewer students to support in his golf coaching business. We tripled the fees for his products, 40% of his old students left, but those who stayed were loyal, his revenue increased by 2.5x immediately and he found he had 37% more time.

This was just the first of many simple frameworks I introduced in my own coaching practice.

I told myself, *"Robin, you need to create a simple pricing framework for coaches like you. They need to increase their fees, work with fewer clients, be more confident about the amazing value they bring to the world...and simply put...stop being a busy fool!"*

Find your coach...

Coaching isn't a new thing. Some 8,000 years ago, within the walls of Babylon, Arkad, a lowly scribe, took advice from a rich man to take 10% of everything he earned and keep it for himself. The rich man went on to give Arkad seven further tips on how to amass wealth.

Thankfully Arkad kept a record of these tips on several clay tablets, the internet of Babylonian times, for our reference.

Arkad went on to become the Richest Man in Babylon and was invited by the Babylonian Government to teach the top 50 teachers in Babylon on how to build wealth, so they could teach more people.
The secret? Wealth didn't come from earning more money, but in learning how to manage their money better.

The people of Babylon had found their coach.

2,500 years ago, the problems of the modern world were being discussed by the greatest thinkers and founders of western philosophy.

The best of those philosophers weren't the ones providing the solutions to those problems.

No! They were ones who probed the problem.

Plato noted a conversation between Socrates and his student Meno:

Socrates: ***Well, does anybody want to be unhappy and unfortunate?***

Meno: ***I suppose not.***

Socrates: ***Then if not, nobody desires what is evil, for what else is unhappiness, but desiring evil things and getting them?***

Meno: ***It looks as if you're right, Socrates.***

Socrates invited Meno to go even deeper into his conscious mind to find a solution inside himself.

Meno found his coach.

Woodrow Wilson turned to a young man for advice during World War 1. The trusted adviser had previously founded the George Washington School of Advertising.

The principles of success and self-confidence were taught in this school. So much so that Woodrow Wilson's adviser sold $100,000 of shares in the school which later led to his adviser's arrest...the school's assets were valued at just $1,200.

That man was Napoleon Hill, credited with writing *Think and Grow Rich* in 1937. What many don't know is that it was Hill's then wife, Rosa Lee Beeland, who wrote most of the content in the book.

Either way, 20 million or so people have since purchased a copy of *Think and Grow Rich.*

20 million people found their coach.

Self-help and motivational gurus are now ten-a-penny. Profiting off the back of *Think and Grow Rich*, regurgitating the models and tools of others, but they're missing one key attribute.

Combining the tools of modern business thinking with the art of asking the thought-provoking questions of Socrates.

This is the true skill required to ensure internal growth in self and external growth in business.

It enabled Napoleon Hill to turn $1,200 of assets into $100,000 of investment.

Whilst totally illegal, and I certainly wouldn't condone anything illegal, it does demonstrate the power of being fearless in business.

Tiger Woods enlisted the help of a swing coach, personal trainer, nutritionist, sleep coach and a mindset coach.

Tiger didn't need just ONE coach, but he found FIVE coaches to help him win 14 Major Championships between 1997 and 2008.

Is it any wonder he flopped after sacking his entire team in 2008 and has struggled to be competitive in ANY tournament since?

In 2003 British Cycling turned to Sir Dave Brailsford to inject some extra performance into British Cycling. Brailsford is credited with championing a philosophy of 'marginal gains' at British Cycling.

The whole principle came from the idea that if you broke down everything you could think of that goes into riding a bike, and then improved it by 1%, you will get a significant increase when you put them all together.

Until Team Sky and Sir Dave Brailsford came along, no British rider had ever won the Tour de France.

Winning a total 8 Olympic Gold Medals and 59 World Championships under Brailsford's direction between 2003 and 2018. With Chris Froome, Sir Bradley Wiggins and Geraint Thomas winning 8 Grand Tours between them.

Both the British Cycling and Sky Cycling Teams have found THEIR coach.

Fast forward to now...

A softly-spoken divorce coach held a secret dream to hit £10k a month. After she found THE coach, she has now turned her little business into a limited company and tripled her marketing budget. After hitting £10k a month, her new dream business will be doing £15k - £20k.

Russ, a golf coach from North Wales was struggling with students drifting in and out of lessons which affected his income.

It transpired he had no products. Russ now has five clearly defined products, offers a 100% money back guarantee on his products, and is charging 3x the going rate for lessons.

Russ found THE coach.

A pet business coach was exhausted from rehabilitation dog walks and working 12-20 hours per day. She turned to coaching to help her tackle the overwhelm.

Within 6 months, she was earning more money from working regular eight-hour days. She'd found HER coach.

Her success rate from implementing the Customer Journey is almost 95% conversion once she talks to people via her telephone consultation. And in less than 12 months, her turnover has increased by 325%.

Just in case you haven't worked out who 'THE COACH' is in all the success stories above - it's *me*! Robin Waite – The Fearless Business Coach.

Whatever type of business you have or whichever niche you choose to coach in, I urge you:

Always be the leader you want to be, keep bringing remarkable insights to your clients, create amazing transformations and most of all, build a sustainable business.

These 7 simple steps will transform your small business, help you dominate your niche and shift how you operate as a business owner

No matter where you are right now, when you learn how to stop focusing on building your business you can BUILD YOUR DREAM BUSINESS

"THINGS ARE MUCH WORSE IN IMAGINATION THAN IN REALITY"

You will make excuses. Your old beliefs will tell you this won't work for you. You will stop you from being successful.

Get out of your way and Just Do It!

The 7-Step Blueprint to Building your Dream Business

There is something which Arkad, Napoleon Hill and Sir David Brailsford all had in common which was that they were willing to stand out from the crowd and not concern themselves with what their competitors were doing.

In short, the way to build your dream small business is to try out things that others have not yet tried.

As a small business owner you will constantly want to compare yourself to others. Not only that but you are also your own worst critic:

How much are others in my niche charging? Are they better than me? Why are they (seemingly) so much more in demand than me? Why did that prospect say, "No!"? Is it me? Are my clients really getting great results?

If you can calm your inner critic, and pay attention to the steps included in the Fearless Business Blueprint then I can guarantee you will create a highly-profitable and impactful small business that will transform your clients' lives for many years to come.

This is the Fearless 7-Step Blueprint

1. Productise Your Service to Better Articulate the Value You Bring to Your Clients
2. Use Goal Focused Pricing to Maximise Your Capacity and Earnings Potential
3. Confidently Charge More by using a Pricing Auction
4. Do One Thing Really Well For One Specific Type of Client
5. Create Predictable Sales Via the 6-Step Sales Formula
6. Implement Rocket Fuel Marketing to Help Clients Find You Time and Time Again
7. Leverage: Build a Fearless Product

Running a small business is an engineering problem. The Fearless Business Blueprint are the 7 steps that help you overcome the problem.

Here's a question for you to ruminate on and help explain why:

You are driving a Fiat 500 (more commonly known as a Fiat Cinqecento). You need to get to your destination faster.

What happens if you add Rocket Fuel to a Fiat 500?

[Answer on the next page … please stop reading now and see if you can figure this out.]

To solve this conundrum, ask some questions and start to whittle it down:

"Does the car really need to go faster?" No.

"If the car has a 500cc engine, can it actually go any faster?" No.

"Is the car a rocket ship?" No.

"Is rocket fuel highly combustible?" Yes.

The most common answer I get to this question is that the Fiat 500 will go faster when you add in rocket fuel. But it simply won't.

I don't actually know what happens as I've never seen the results first hand. I can only imagine that, as rocket fuel is highly combustible and the Fiat 500 engine is somewhat rickety, it's unlikely to have a happy ending and will inevitably result in some kind of explosion.

How is this relevant to a Small Business?

In this analogy the Fiat 500 engine represents your own business' engine; the sales, processes, systems, finance, people, marketing etc. And the rocket fuel represents more clients.

Most small businesses can "wing their way to 85k" - the VAT threshold here in the UK, however their business engine is rickety and has limited capacity.

Eventually as you add more clients into your small business the wheels will start to fall off and you risk blowing up your business engine.

The only challenge is we can't predict whether it will be the 12th, 17th or 21st client you enrol.

Rocket fuel is designed for rocket engines...so let's turn your business into a finely tuned rocket engine.

If you succeed at implementing just ONE of the 7 Steps, you'll make a decent living without blowing up your small business.

If you can resolve two or three, your business will be a highly profitable engine which will be more fun to run, far more fulfilling and most importantly more profitable than you could ever imagine.

But first you have to understand why having MORE CLIENTS will NOT help to grow your small business.

To explain this there are three major shifts which have happened in the last 20 years which have broken people's perceptions of marketing and how to grow a business:

Shift #1	**12x Increase in Local Competition** In 2004, when I registered my first Limited Company here in the UK, there were just 468,000 registered small businesses. In 2025 there are 6,000,000 registered small businesses - a more than 12-fold increase. Which means 12x the accountants, 12x the business coaches, 12x the web designers...you name it, you have far more competition in your local, geographical area. All competing for a similar amount of business.
Shift #2	**Fast Internet in the early 2000s** Yes, fast internet has enabled numerous things, streaming TV, access to websites and information, and millions of apps. But it's also been the catalyst for a Global Marketplace. Whilst it's never been easier to get online and start a business, you're no longer competing against your local, geographical neighbours but hundreds of millions of small businesses globally.
Shift #3	**Rapid Expansion of Social Media in the 2010s** In 2014, few people were using social media, even fewer knew how to leverage it for their small business but, for those who did, it was like the Goldrush in the Wild West. As more people saw successful online marketeers having enormous successes, everyone piled onto Facebook, LinkedIn, X, Instagram and now TikTok.

These three shifts have left social media hugely over-saturated and most people's approaches seem to be to walk to the edge of the void and shout into the abyss:

"Buy my sh*t! Buy my sh*t! Buy my Sh*t!"

The Dream Business...a Fearless Business...

Is one where you have half the clients but double the income.

My invitation to you is to commit to the 7 Steps in this Blueprint for the next 12 months.

What will the future version of you be looking back on you doing today and thanking you for?

7 Steps to Fearless Business

How to Grow a Fearless Business in 30 Days or Less While Enrolling Fewer Clients and Doing Less Marketing

Here are the essential steps to building a Fearless Business based on sustainability and profitability, building your future security and removing fear in the process.

STEP 1 Productise Your Service to Better Articulate the Value You Bring to Your Clients

Like most business owners, you had a great idea and, encouraged by a friend or loved one, launched into business and after reviewing your competitors' prices, started charging an hourly rate.

This is a flawed business model, not to mention borderline unethical, and will likely be losing you a lot of money.

STEP 2 Use Goal-Focused Pricing to Maximise Your Capacity and Your Earnings Potential

Out of an assessment of 1,218 business owners, 26.4% people rated their business plan a 1/10, basically non-existent.

And as they say, "Fail to plan = planning to fail!".

Seven simple questions will lead to you building a bulletproof 1-page business plan to achieve your dream financial goals.

STEP 3 Confidently Charge More By Using a Pricing Auction

Earn Double Your Income With Half the Clients

Instead of getting stuck in the Sales Cycle of Doom, it's far better to raise your prices.

This gives you more time to deliver a better quality product to your clients, which gets them better results, and makes you more money on the backend as well as generating more referrals.

STEP 4 Do One Thing Really Well For One Specific Type of Client

Be The Standout Expert in Your Niche

Instead of being a Jack of all Trades and a master at none, the most successful businesses have learned to do one thing really well for one specific type of client. This immediately positions you as an expert in your niche.

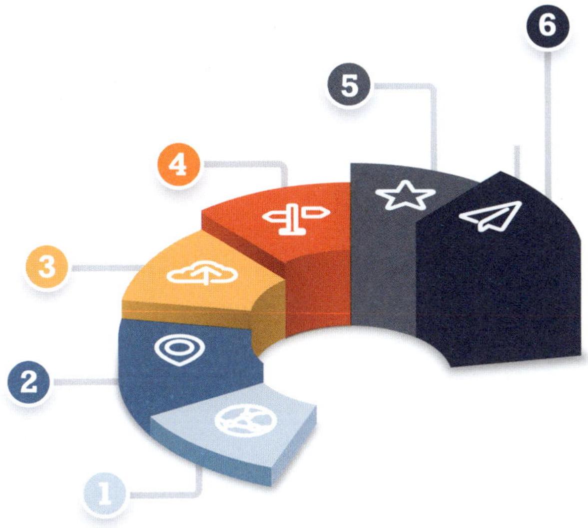

STEP 5 Create Predictable Sales via The 6-Step Sales Formula

The Simplest and Only Sales Framework You'll Ever Need

Once we've improved your offer and doubled your prices, you're going to have to improve your sales game. A 90% conversion rate is no longer acceptable. We want to LOWER your conversion rate.

Yes, you'll get better at sales and end up with fewer, higher-paying clients because you'll understand why qualifying prospects is so important in building a Fearless Business.

STEP 6 Implement Rocket Fuel Marketing to Help Clients Find You Time and Time Again

Build $100k+ Partnerships with Fun, Influential Creators in Far Less Time

Social media is like the Noah's Ark of the marketing world, 1-by-1-by-1. Imagine if you could guest on a single podcast and generate over 3,000 leads and $300k in new business. This is possible when you understand the right way to build meaningful partnerships with influential people.

STEP 7 Leverage (Build a Fearless Product)

Create a Something Which is 5x More Expensive Than Your Most Expensive Product

There is a reason why Ferrari can sell expensive cars and Rolex can sell expensive watches. They know that there is an audience out there for premium products. They don't build the product first and then try to sell it. They know that 4% of their clients are looking for a premium solution.

STEP 1 Productise Your Service to Better Articulate Your Value to Your Clients

At Fearless HQ the words, "It depends!" are swear words and immediately invoke a fine and when I hear these immortal words, generally it tells me that the business owner in front of me is charging hourly rates and struggles to define who their ideal client is, what they can do for them, how long it is going to take or how much they are going to charge.

The goal of Productising Your Service is to create a small suite of 3-5 hero products which satisfy 90% of your ideal clients' needs.

The first step in Productising a Service?

For many years I set out to be a creator, to be different, to have unique selling propositions and find ways to stand out in a hugely oversaturated market of coaches.

I failed miserably.

I stand before you today (metaphorically) a hero of my own abject lack of success at standing out.

And yet…I *DO* stand out.

The penny dropped when I realised that I'd made standing out all about me. When I shifted my perspective onto what I do for my coaching clients and how I help them to stand out, my world shifted.

My own business is in fact very boring!

The first step in Productising a Service is to leave your own ego at the door. Your desire to build custom 'this' and bespoke 'that' is driven by your own neediness to be an artist, but it is not important to your customers. All it does is stroke your own ego. What your clients care about is, "What's in it for them?"

A Productised Service Doesn't Have to Be Boring

Apple has done a brilliant job of producing a small number of beautiful products. They have 5 hero products; the iPhone, the Mac/Macbook, the iPad, the Apple Watch and AirPods. The products are sleek, robust, beautiful, technologically advanced, but can

you imagine if Apple had to create 232,000,000 bespoke iPhones every year? It would never happen.

Apple knows that if people don't like their phones they can go and buy a Samsung. Apple has production lines, where thousands of iPhones are churned out every day, the same components being added every day being packaged in the same boxes every day.

Apple, behind the scenes, is one of THE most boring businesses going. Yet on the surface Apple feels like a very exciting business and Apple's products are adored by billions of people.

Make a Boring Service Fun

The marine engineer is called in to fix a faltering engine on an oil tanker. He arrives by helicopter and the captain shows the engineer down to the engine room. The engineer walks around the engine room knocking on bits of metal and putting his ear up against the pipes.

He pulls out a hammer, strikes the engine, which immediately fires back into life.

A week later the captain receives an email containing an invoice for $100,000. The captain, incensed, asks the engineer to explain the invoice.

To which he replies, "$100 to hit the engine with a hammer, $99,900 to know where to hit it!"

This sounds fun, hitting things with hammers, getting predictable results and getting paid large sums of money. Well, fun to me!

When is an Hour not an Hour?

The answer to this riddle is simple, when it's given to someone who is incompetent.This is where service providers get very hung up by the differences between products and services. A service is traditionally an exchange of time-for-money whereas a product has a clearly defined set of features.

I genuinely believe that time-for-money is an unethical and irresponsible way to charge people.

Let me give you an example of three web designers (Spot the clues that hourly rates just don't work..?)

	Dave	Vijay	Kerry
Experience	Very little	8 Years (Doesn't know what Robin knows about pricing)	30 years Website Ninja
Charges	$50/hr	$50/hr	$10,000
Promises	A website, roughly 20 hours in about a month	An SEO optimised website with a shopping cart and blog in less than 7 days, total build time 10 hours	72 hours 12-15 fully qualified leads per month and within 30 days
Delivers	3 months later, forgets the blog and shopping cart, website looks like a dog's dinner	As promised, very professionally designed, gets found in Google… but no enquiries	First qualified lead within 24 hrs of website going live. Tells you there's no need for a shopping cart or blog.
Challenges	You ask for the blog and shopping cart, Dave tells you it will take 10 more hours, you're not happy	A slight hiccup moving hosting over, aside from that it seems good.	None, in fact you have TOO MANY leads coming in now.
Money-Back Guarantee	Dave's already spent your money on a new BMW	Vijay will keep working until you're happy but confident in his rates so keeps charging $50/hr for updates	15 qualified leads a month or your money back + $1,000 for wasting your time
Total Cost	$1,500	$500	$10,000
ROI	Minus $1,500 + an extra $1k to Vijay to fix the issues	Minus $1k but you can see some potential and leads are trickling in. Maybe $20k per year.	$100k in the first month, the leads are good and predictable. In fact so much so you sign up to Kerry's Platinum Ad Campaigns to drive even more traffic at $5k/mth

Clue #1 - Vijay, despite his greater experience, gets paid less than Dave for doing a superior piece of work. Our first clue that hourly rates are a flawed charging model.

Clue #2 - Dave is resentful at having to do the extra work, reluctantly doing it for free, but the mere fact he could bump on extra hours again is a clue that hourly rates are a flawed charging model.

Clue #3 - Kerry doesn't charge for her time, she is solely focused on client results, so much so that she has a cast-iron moneyback guarantee. Kerry charged a fixed fee for her work, turns it around in 72 hourrs and focuses on getting her client an ROI within 30 days.Despite the seemingly inflated price tag this is easily the best option.

The 3 Steps to Productising Your Service:

Define The Dream Outcome your clients get when they work with you is the key to Productising Your Service.

When Elon Musk sells his Teslas, they don't sell a list of features like the torque of the motors, the number of doors the cars have or the tension in the suspension springs.

No, they tell you a Tesla will do 0-60mph in 3.6 seconds. How are you going to feel when you get in and hit the accelerator for the first time?

What is the Dream Outcome you deliver for your clients?

Your clients don't buy websites, they buy enquiries and sales.

Your customers don't want therapy, they want to feel happy and confident again.

Your clients don't want coaching, they want to have a confident sales conversation and sell their services for more money.

Deliver Results Within a Pre-Agreed Time Frame so that your clients know exactly when they are likely to see results.

Ask yourself this question, *"How long does it take, on average, for your clients to see results?"*

If you are a coach who helps entrepreneurs with their confidence. And it typically takes 8-12 weeks to see results. Make your programme a 12 Week Transformation Programme. 90% of people will fit in the middle of the bell curve. If they don't, narrow down your ideal client (see Step 4).

Diffusion of Innovation

Source: Everett Rogers

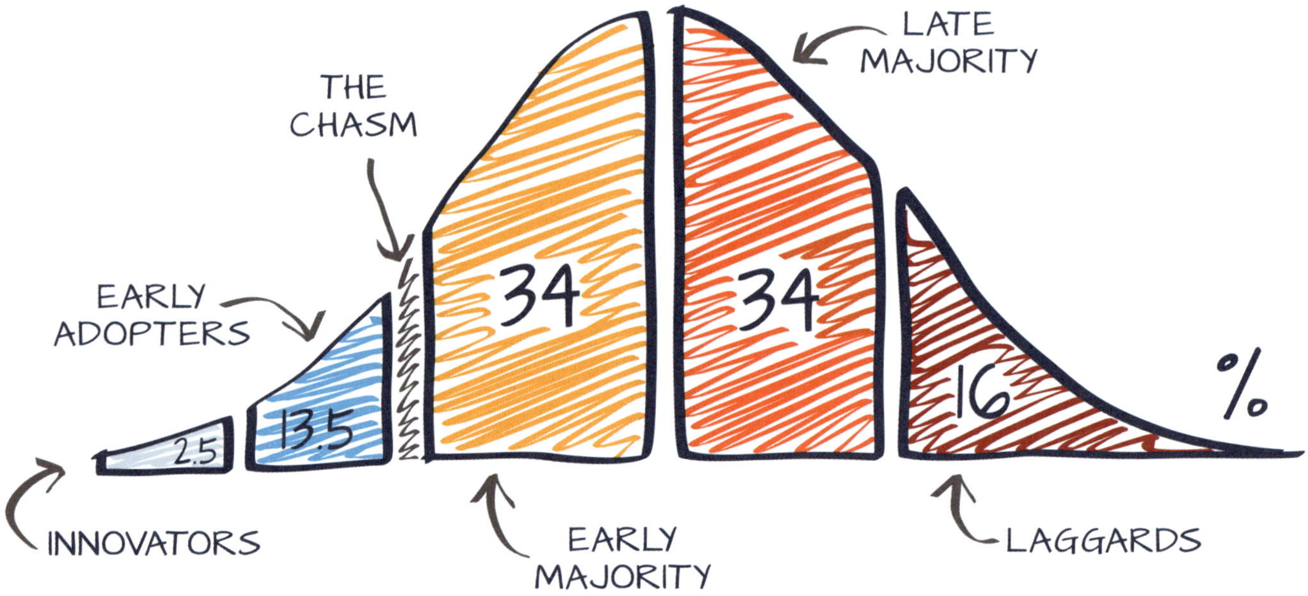

ACTION STEPS

1. Define the Dream Outcome or Results that your product offers.

2. Determine the "average" amount of time it takes to deliver that outcome to your "average" client.

3. Assign a fixed fee for delivering those results to your clients.

FURTHER STUDY: Read ***Take Your Shot*** so you can understand the full process of productising a service.

Scan the QR code for a FREE signed copy.

www.fearless.biz/tys

Even if you are charging an hourly rate, start to get comfortable saying "the big number". For example if you are a coach charging $100 per session, and your client experiences their transformation in 12 weeks (on average) with a weekly session. Try selling a package for $1,200 instead. Get comfortable saying the big number. Commit to pitch at least 10 prospective clients $1,200 for your 12-Week Transformation programme.

Another good question would be, "What if I had to offer a 100% moneyback guarantee if I don't deliver within a certain time frame?"

Did I hear you mutter, "It depends, Robin!" to yourself. This means you likely do too many different things for too many different people i.e. you have too many variables within your business. And therefore it is unpredictable. Do your clients want unpredictable results? I doubt it. Push your ego aside and build a boring business which produces predictable results within a predictable time frame.

Your task is to remove the variables so your results become more predictable. And the key word here is "average".

Charge a fixed fee so your clients no longer have to guess how long it is going or how much it will cost to work with you before they start seeing results.

Again, I can tell what you're thinking, "But every client is different, Robin, how can I set a fixed fee?"

True, every client is different, but only because you are enrolling lots of different types of clients. Imagine if all your clients were similar?

There's a chance you're charging time-for-money, hour or day rates, similar to your competitors.

So you feel you'll lose out financially if the service takes longer to deliver especially if your clients are difficult.

If you do the same thing for similar clients will the time to see results for your clients start to become more predictable?

Yes, because you are doing the same thing, over and over again, for similar clients.

This means you will get better at it and do it faster.

Therefore you should get paid MORE, not less.

It is your responsibility to qualify your clients before you work with them. Properly vetted, you will start to discern which ones are the best clients and you can get good results for.

Figure out what their problems, pain points and challenges are and how much they will spend to have those problems and pains taken away from them. Charge accordingly to create that result.

Hint: Having worked with 2,500 clients over nine years, when clients have learned how to productise their service they typically end up charging 2.4x their previous hourly rate for the same product or service.

STEP 2 Goal Focused Pricing to Maximise Your Capacity and Earnings Potential

Thanks to fast-internet and a global marketplace it's never been easier to get online and start a business. You don't even need a coach or mentor any more because AI will answer most of your questions!

Yet many small business owners, working 40+ hours per week, get to the end of the month and scratch their heads wondering why there's little money left to pay themselves.

Truth is, 76% of small business owners have a great idea for their business but don't have a great business for their idea.

This is the simplest 1-Page Business Plan framework you'll ever find, it's also known as "Goal-Focused Pricing" and will provide a simple north star for your business no matter where you are on your journey.

It will help identify your capacity, how many clients you need to achieve your financial goals, how much to sell your products/services for, how many sales calls you'll need to make and even how many leads to generate.

Your 1-Page Business Plan will help identify the following metrics:

Target Revenue: How much income you would like to bring into your business in the next 12 months?

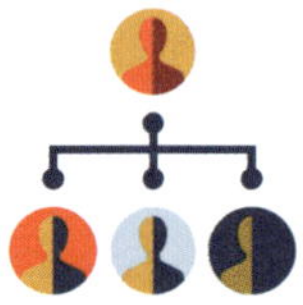

Your Capacity: The precise number of clients or customers that you can realistically serve each week/month/year.

Product Price: How much the average sale is worth to your business when you enrol a new customer

Sales Meetings: How many sales calls/ consultations you need to sit each week to fill up your capacity.

Lead Flow: How many leads or prospects you need to attract into your pipeline to convert into sales.

Weekly Activity: The minimum amount of activity you need to be doing each week to achieve all of the above targets.

1-Page Business Plan Example

By answering nine simple questions you will be able to work out five important metrics your business needs (like oxygen) to achieve your very own Fearless Business: Turnover; Average Selling Price, Capacity (that is, the number of clients you can serve), Consultations and Leads.

Have a go at completing your own 1-Page Fearless Business Plan on the next page.

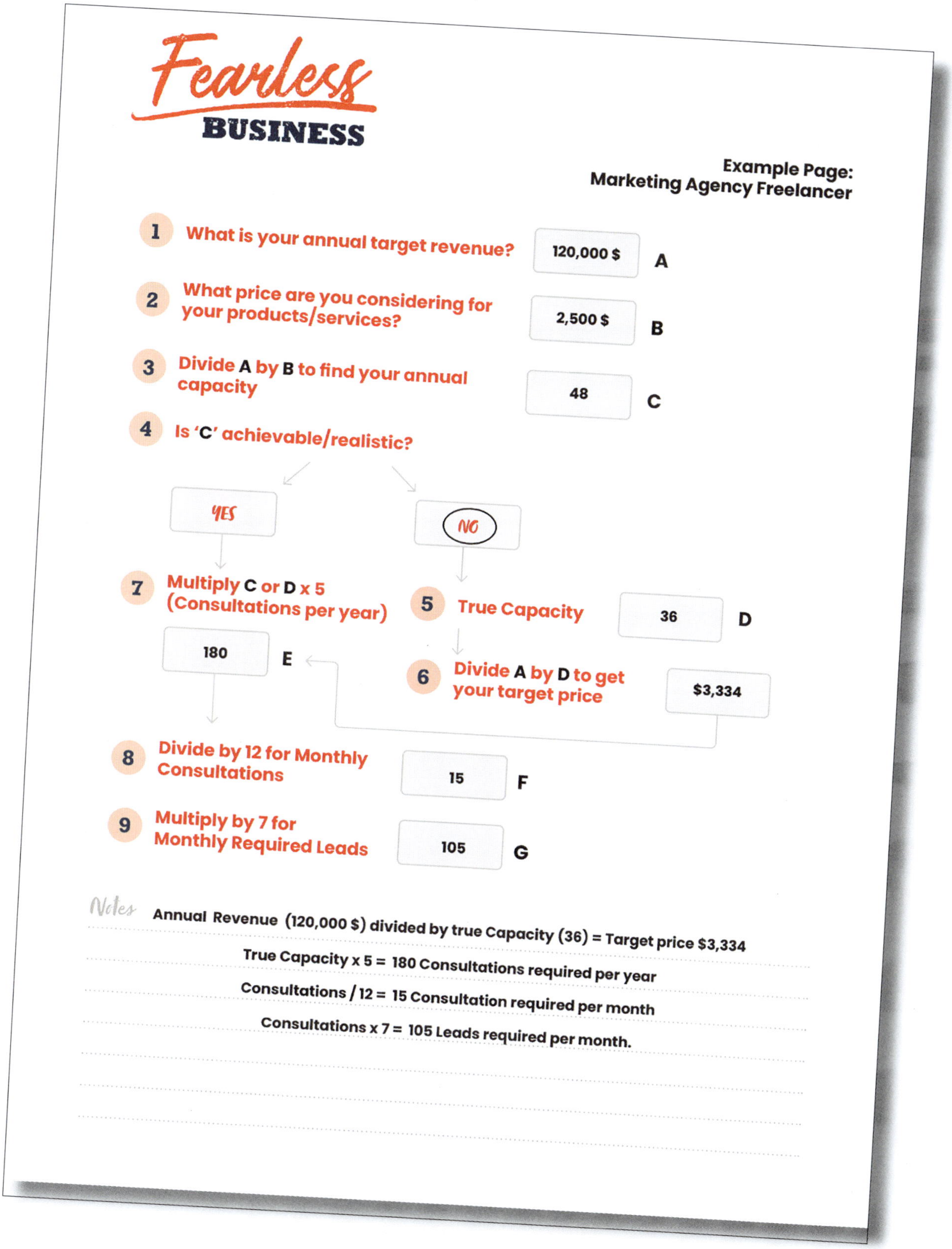

Fearless BUSINESS

Example Page:
Marketing Agency Freelancer

1. What is your annual target revenue? — 120,000 $ — A
2. What price are you considering for your products/services? — 2,500 $ — B
3. Divide A by B to find your annual capacity — 48 — C
4. Is 'C' achievable/realistic?

YES / NO (circled: NO)

5. True Capacity — 36 — D
6. Divide A by D to get your target price — $3,334
7. Multiply C or D x 5 (Consultations per year) — 180 — E
8. Divide by 12 for Monthly Consultations — 15 — F
9. Multiply by 7 for Monthly Required Leads — 105 — G

Notes

Annual Revenue (120,000 $) divided by true Capacity (36) = Target price $3,334

True Capacity x 5 = 180 Consultations required per year

Consultations / 12 = 15 Consultation required per month

Consultations x 7 = 105 Leads required per month.

Fearless
BUSINESS

1. What is your annual target revenue? **A**

2. What price are you considering for your products/services? **B**

3. Divide **A** by **B**, to give your annual capacity, **C** **C**

4. Is **C** achievable/realistic?

Yes | No

7. Multiply **C** or **D** x 5 (Consultations per year)

E

5. True capacity **D**

6. Divide **A** by **D** to get your target price

8. Divide **E** by 12 for monthly consultations **F**

9. Multiply **F** by 7 for required monthly leads **G**

Notes

Your 1-Page Fearless Business Plan <<<

Just follow these simple instructions and fill in *your* plan, left.

1. What is your target revenue for the next 12 months? **A**
2. What is the "average" selling price of your products/services? **B**
3. Now, divide your answer for **A** by **B**, this gives your capacity, **C**
4. Is **C** achievable/realistic?

   If **Yes** *- Multiply* **C** *x 5 to get the number of consultations per year =* **E**

   If **No** *- What is a more realistic number of clients/customers you can work with?*
5. True capacity = **D**.
6. Divide **A** by **D** = The price you need to aim for. Then mutiply x 5 again = **E**

   A good conversion rate is 1:3 to 1:5 - let's work on the worst-case scenario, 1:5.
7. **C** x **D** = **E** the number of consultations you need to sit over the next 12 months
8. Divide **E** by 12 to get **F** - the number of sales calls or consultations per month that you need to sit.
9. Take **F** and multiply it by 7. This is the number of leads you need to generate each month with prospective clients.

ACTION STEPS

1. Define the Dream Outcome or Start with the end in mind and then reverse engineer the perfect business model for you.

2. If your capacity is limited you may need to consider raising your prices. This signals to the market that you are exclusive.

3. Be clear on your weekly activity. Create a perfect repeatable week to achieve your long-term financial goals

FURTHER STUDY: Need some help with the above exercise? Scan the QR code to watch the 1-Page Business Plan Video Guide.

youtube.com/RobinMWaite

Remember, the goal in business is not to enrol as many clients as you can, the goal is to build a profitable and sustainable business. In an ideal world you need to design your business so you have double the income with half the clients.

STEP 3 Confidently Charge More by using a Pricing Auction

99.9% of the human population haven't grown up with a trust fund or a silver spoon in their mouths. They are humble and proud, happy to work hard, take the odd risk and maybe even build something great.

Every one of you will have a different money story and money mindset. You will have different thoughts, feelings and attachments to money. You will remember your story about money growing up. For some it will be very positive. For the vast majority, not so much.

Arguments which raged in homes between parents and family members around money have a lasting effect on the vast majority of small business owners. Likely before your earliest memories were even formed you will have already developed your earliest attachments to money.

Do you remember hearing things like:

"Money doesn't grow on trees!"

"Money is the root of all evil!"

"Look at their car, that's disgusting how much money they have!"

"We don't go on holidays, because we can't afford it!"

"You can't have those shoes, Robin, because we've got no money!"

Followed by shouting, and banging and, perhaps, doors slamming?

Can you see how toxic all of these statements are?

What is your money story? What can you remember from your childhood growing up?

Then you get older, a teenager, and is it any wonder that your pocket money, paper-round money and the money you earned waiting tables came and went easily.

You became a student or left home, then money came even more easily in the form of credit cards, student loans and in some cases maybe even a mortgage.

All the while, scarcity very quickly followed abundance.

You try to break out, set up a business.

"This will give me my freedom!" you think.

Yet the same problems persist.

You don't have a cashflow problem

The money flows in…and flows straight back out again.

You don't have a cashflow problem at all, actually you have two other problems:

A making more money problem.

And a keeping that money problem.

These are the essential two habits to learn, implement and practice throughout your business' lifespan.

Add into the mix some of the toxic traits and beliefs around money that you developed in your childhood and bring them into your adult life, now running a small business - perhaps you can now see how they are not serving you.

Making More Money Is Hard

Let's look specifically at you, your business and the idea of making more money.

You are smart. You work hard, earning a good hourly or day rate.

You get amazing results for your clients. And on the whole you enjoy the work you are doing.

Yet, you get to the end of the month and scratch your head wondering where all the money is.

Don't get me wrong, your mortgage is paid, you have food on your table and a nice holiday each year, but everyone promised you more!

The reality is most, coaches, consultants and freelancers base their earnings on working a traditional working week of 37.5 hours.

Charge $50/hr and you should be able to bring in $1,875 a week.

Your dream of $10k months is now shattered. $1,875 x 4.2 weeks per month = just $7,875.

Your earnings potential is now capped because of time and money constraints. You raise your fees to $80/hr. Now you could earn $12,600 per month but it's still a struggle.

Well, you have children so you can deduct six weeks of holiday each year, you get ill and your children get ill, plus you have to do school drop-off and pick-up... and the 37.5 hrs now feels more like 25 hrs/wk.

The networking meeting you go to each week, that's another 3 hours. 1-2 sales calls per week, another two hours, writing proposals for said meetings, another four hours. And so on. You get the picture.

Most small business owners only realistically have 2-2.5 revenue generating days per week and this is why making more money feels hard as a small business owner.

Keeping the Money You Make

The experts, coaches and mentors all tell you to "outsource" your non-revenue generating work to create more time for you to earn more.

They require time for managing and training, for questions, and don't forget they're non-revenue generating so you now have two or more mouths to feed. You still have to do sales meetings and proposals and networking meetings and the school run. They can't do those things.

So what's left? Social media and your accounts? Well social media's not working out for you and your accounts take about five minutes a day.

You hire a marketing manager at $50/hr, someone to help you create and edit videos at $25/hr, and an email marketing expert on $100/email (notice they're all marketing activities) and a bookkeeper on $40/hr. It kind of works. You've got more money coming in and you're working all hours to service those clients. You're exhausted and feeling burned out...and still don't have any significant profits because you spent it on all the other non-revenue generating tasks in your business.

There are two important principles to understand when setting your prices:

Principle 1 - Pricing Bandwidth

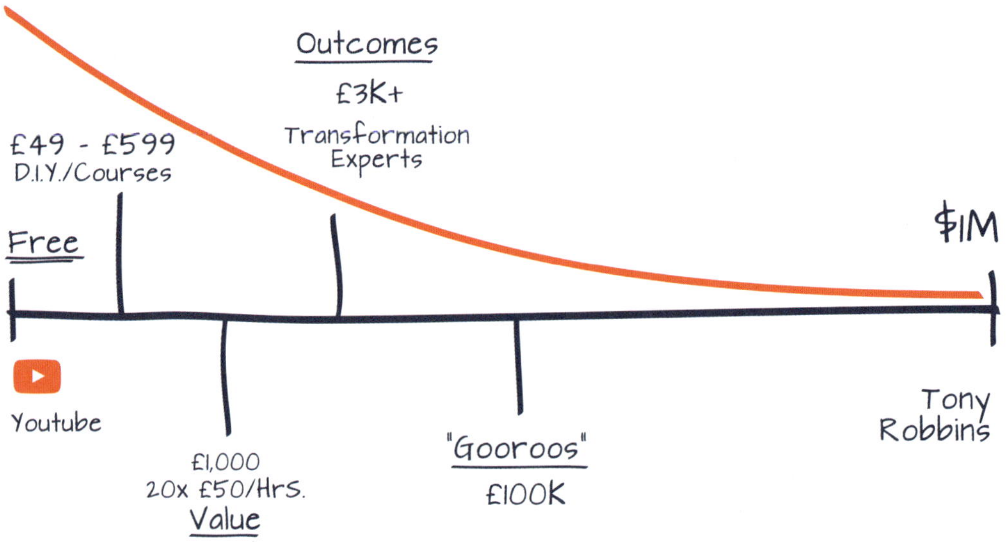

Most people see pricing as "binary", it's either; too cheap or too expensive, it's a "Heck yes!" or a, "Hell no!", or an, "I'm in!" or, "I'm out!".

Whereas the reality is pricing operates along a "bandwith". On this bandwidth line the same product might be sold by three different people. One selling it at $300, the second at $500 and the third is selling it for $800.

And they will ALL have customers who are interested in buying their product because they feel it is fair value or have other customers who will tell them it's too cheap and/or too expensive.

How can the $300 product be too cheap AND too expensive when compared to the $800 product which people also believe to be too cheap AND too expensive?

It's all down to the notion of a fair exchange.

Provided there are more people wanting to buy a product than there are products available to buy then this will drive prices up. And some service providers will naturally be more in demand because of their personal branding and marketing activities than others.

The temptation is to try to stimulate demand by lowering your prices.

This signals to the market that there is an infinite amount of supply of your product.

When there's lots of something available, is it more or less attractive? I'd say, less attractive.

By raising the price of your products you are signalling to the market that you are exclusive and supply of your product is limited, which drives demand up instead of down.

It's why, in the coaching world for example, the same information is available on a bandwidth of FREE to millions of dollars:

Free - YouTube videos, easy to search and access, millions of videos, most of them mediocre at best, but search enough and you'll find a good one.

$49-297 - DIY courses, more structured and organised, maybe a bit of access to the creator for some extra help and/or a community.

$200/hr or session - Value based coaching when you buy an hour of the coach's time and extract as much value from them as you can. Lots of available sessions.

$3-5k package - They offer a specific transformation over a fixed period of time and for a fixed fee. Limited capacity to 20 clients per year.

$100k - The "gooroos", significant demand, very limited spaces available for coaching.

$1m - The Tony Robbins effect where there is only one Tony and millions of people want him. Esther Perelle. Or other similar celebrity experts and coaches.

All of these people and solutions do the same thing, coaching, but the value is determined by demand.

And if you look at the attached chat…the more you charge, then the less competition their is in your chosen pricing niche.

Principle 2 - Sales Cycle of Doom

I don't know which idiot made up the rule that the goal in business was to attract as many clients into your business as humanly possible, but it seems pervasive in the small business community.

The real goal in business is to build a profitable and sustainable business.

Blindly enrolling as many clients as possible into a business is ok, only when the business model has proved sustainable and profitable. When a business lacks profit and you try to grow your way out of the problem through enrolling more clients all that you are doing is scaling a problem.

What this sounds like for a business which isn't profitable is a constant cycle of:

Sell > Deliver > Sell > Deliver

And so on. Time flies by.

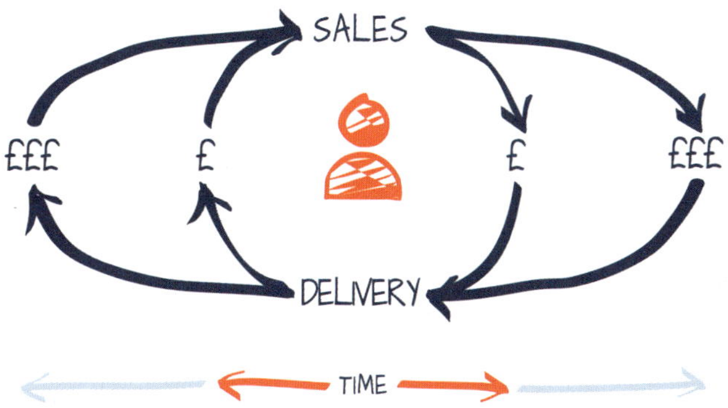

Results feel perennially unachievable. Until finally you burn out, take a holiday or your children get sick. Then you stop for a bit. Take a deep breath and then start all over again. This Sales Cycle of Doom ruins business owners.

It is far better to slow down the Sales Cycle of Doom by raising your prices.

This creates a virtuous cycle.

More money up front > more time to deliver a better quality product/service > better client results and outcomes > makes you more referable > makes you more money > and gives you far less stress.

Yes, fewer clients equals a far better business.

A Fearless Business is one with double the income and half the clients.

Exercise - The Pricing 'Auction'

When we try to solve a pricing problem we typically solve it intellectually. Meaning that we use some maths, thinking about what we think people will pay, look at our competitors and then bring them altogether to decide on a price.

However, research suggests that while nearly everyone believes they are self-aware, only about 10 to 15% of people are genuinely self-aware.

Therefore there is also some subconscious psychology at play too.

Think about the last big purchase you made. You saved up your hard earned money. And finally booked that dream holiday, bought your dream car or maybe a lovely watch or piece of jewellery as a reward to yourself for all your hard work.

When you finally made the purchase, was it an intellectual decision? Or were you just super excited? Maybe even experienced a bit of buyer's remorse afterwards? That's the psychology at play. All purchasing decisions are based on 90% emotions and 10% cognitive thought process.

It is the same when you are selling something.

Of all the coaching work I get to do this is one of my favourite exercises with clients.

Step 1: You are going to write down one of your existing products or services and ascertain a price point you think is about the right amount to charge for it.

Step 2: You are going to gradually increase the price of your product. I find that when you get into 4-figures then 2's, 5's and 8's are significant.

Step 3: Get woo!! Listen to your body. As you write the numbers down, when you feel that knot in your stomach you've likely just gone outside your comfort zone.

That is the price your subconscious thinks you should be charging. Typically when I do this exercise people end up, on average, at 2.5 times their original product price.

In the example below, Prices 1-3 felt comfortable, there was a little resistance at $2,800 and a LOT of resistance at $3,200. Crossing the $3k mark became uncomfortable for the person doing the exercise.

You have a go…

I Have a Bet For You...

...which I have NEVER lost!

Yes, I've thrown down the gauntlet.

Have you settled upon a higher price point after doing the exercise above? If not, then you might want to. Simply double your old fee if you're unsure because, trust me, you are going to want to take this bet!

Decide on whether you like to play just inside your comfort zone or just outside it.

Once you've made a decision on your new price point. You must commit to pitching your next ten prospective clients at your new fee, and on a sales call…no more hiding behind proposals!

You literally cannot lose this bet!

Here is the bet - if you can document your process of pitching those ten prospects (recording your conversations ideally) and you don't close ANY of the ten, then I will buy your product at your new price point.

All I ask is that if you get five pitches in and have no conversions you email me and let me know. I will then give you a free 30 minute sales coaching call. And we will role-play the conversations.

Yes, basically I want to swing the odds in my favour a little bit, which I feel is fair.

Either way, you cannot lose. Either you close a client at a higher price point or I will be your first customer at the new price point.

Deal? My personal email is - robin@robinwaite.com

The Product or Package	**Example** A website design starter package	**Your Go…**
Hourly Rate	$80/hr	
Hours	20	
Price	$1,600	
Price 1	$1,800	
Price 2	$2,200	
Price 3	$2,500	
Price 4	$2,800	
Price 5	$3,200	
Price 6	-	
Price 7	-	

ACTION STEPS

1. First of all, acknowledge that hourly and day rates are a flawed business model.

Most importantly, you have to accept that you are selling yourself short and admit that your fees are too cheap.

2. Secondly, get really comfortable selling packages.

Do fewer things for fewer people.

On sales calls, get confident saying the big number.

3. Go through the auction with yourself. Raise your fees until you get that knot in your stomach that you have stretched your prices just outside your comfort zone.

Commit to pitching the next 10 prospects at that new price.

FURTHER STUDY: Need some help with the above exercise? Scan the QR code to apply for a FREE Coaching Session with Robin.

www.robinwaite.com/app

You cannot make more money unless you start asking for it. Take up Robin on his bet. He has never lost this bet. You literally cannot lose. Clients pay Robin thousands of pounds to learn this process and it is practiced daily by Robin's clients.

STEP 4 Do One Thing Really Well For One Specific Type of Client

I recognise that marketeers are going to be reading this, and it's likely that if that's you, then you may wish to skip this paragraph as you may not like what I'm about to share with you.

Marketeers are very good at selling "strategy" but rarely question your business model.

How this shows up in the world is:

The LinkedIn gooroo will tell you to double down on LinkedIn personal branding...

The Instagram superstar will get you started posting 19 reels per day...

The website aficionado will sell you the most beautifully-designed brochure style website and...

The ads expert will insist on you investing into a 3-6 month Google/Meta/LinkedIn/TikTok Ad campaign...

Market Niche

DEMOGRAPHICS - Clever marketeers will invite you to describe your ideal client avatar. Unfortunately most only scratch the surface in describing their clients in terms of gender, age, geographical location and industry. They might go a little bit deeper and start to look at their behaviours.

PSYCHOGRAPHICS: Far more informative as this describes how, why and where your ideal client shows up in the world. What magazines do they subscribe and read? What podcasts do they listen to? Which events do they attend? If you know who your ideal client is and where they show up in the world you stand a far better chance of attracting them and enrolling them as clients.

IDENTITY: This layer is what tribes and villages were built on. Like attracts like. I'll bet, if you look at your existing clients and people you hang out with, there are some remarkable similarities between you. Once you know who you are you can find people who are similar who would make dream clients.

Finally, there are three important questions to ask yourself before taking on ANY client:

Who do you love working with the most? You don't enrol clients unless they are a 9/10 or more. Choose only to work with people you are passionate about helping. Remember that time you took on a client just for the money? Were they just a 5/10? With hindsight you may not have taken them on

Who do you get the best results for? This is tricky, you may love a client but find them difficult to work with and results hard to come by. You want happy clients who will get great results and then refer you to their colleagues. If you only get 7/10 results for them do you think they will refer you?

Who can afford to work with you? You may love the clients and get great results for them but if getting paid is like extracting blood from a stone then resentment will eventually start to build. Purposefully look to attract and enrol clients who have a budget for the amazing work which you do.

Product Niche

Packaging up your offer is simple…but small business owners are great at making things complicated. If you give a 2-hour task eight hours the likelihood is you're very good at making the task four times more complex to fill up the time.

Your job as an entrepreneur is to simplify your business and remove as many variables as you possibly can do.

If you want to corner your Product Niche you need to create a suite of 3-5 Core Products which satisfy 90% of your ideal clients' needs.

If you hear yourself saying, "It depends!" to yourself, that's a sign there are too many variables. It's time to simplify and remove complexity.

How to Productise Your Service in three simple steps:

RESULTS: Definite a Dream Outcome. What full and remarkable outcome or result does your Core Product deliver? You must create a product which is teachable, learnable and repeatable. That can be systemised and process driven. One that you can do time and again for different clients and the SAME RESULT happens predictably each time you deliver it for every client.

TIMEFRAME: Have you ever experienced someone charging you by the hour and you find yourself to be one of those slightly annoying clients regularly asking, "How much longer is this going to take?" Would you rather be told exactly when your product (or the result of the product) is going to be delivered? Again, if you are muttering to yourself, "It depends! It depends on the clients, they're all different, I want to imprint my creative flair on this project…" then you are doing it wrong. You need a dream repeatable results machine where it takes the same amount of time to deliver the results you are promising your clients. Ideally measured in days, weeks or months.

FIXED FEE: There is nothing worse that scope creep in a project. How much does the average client spend with you? Double that number and charge that as a fixed fee to your clients. Now you've got skin in the game to deliver a full and remarkable solution that gets results.

Pricing Niche

When you nail your Market Niche and your Pricing Niche and figure out how to "Do ONE thing really well for ONE specific client" then you will become known as the expert in your niche and can therefore command whatever Pricing Niche you choose.

Rarely do marketeers ask you questions like:

What is your current revenue? And what is your dream monthly revenue?

What is your current cost-per-lead, cost per acquisition and conversion rate?

How much does the average client spend with you?

How many times does the average client repeat -purchase from you?

What (or who) is your biggest bottleneck in your business right now?

Do you really need (or want to) do LinkedIn/Ads/ Instagram/Reels/YouTube?
(Delete as appropriate).

Rarely will they help you work out your ROI (Return on Investment) when you work with them.

They will definitely NEVER ask themselves if you definitely 100% need their services or not.

It's implied that you do.

When you understand what I'm about to share with you about Niching. You can answer all of these questions yourself and determine whether your money will be well spent or not.

ACTION STEPS

1. Write out the key Demographics, Psychographics, and Identity of your ideal client.

Be exclusive and choose to only work with clients who fit this brief.

2. It's time to be really clear about how you help people.

Define the Dream Outcome that THEY are looking for, deliver it over a Clearly Defined Timeframe and for a Fixed Fee.

3. It's time to position yourself as the Expert.

There can only be one who is the most expensive in the market so why isn't you?

FURTHER STUDY: I have created two worksheets. Use the ones opposite or download the full page versions if you need more rows with the QR code.

Email me if you can't access the sheets robin@robinwaite.com

WHICH IDEA...?

Write out ALL your ideas in the first column (don't analyse yet)

WHICH NICHE...?

Write out ALL your potential ideal client avatars/niches in the first column (don't analyse yet).

For both exercises: Go down each 'criteria' column and grade the potential of each niche or idea from 1 to 10. You can create your own spreadsheet and add your own criteria if you want to.

DO NOT overthink these exercises, go with your gut instinct.

Add up the TOTAL scores in the last column. Colour code the rows **RED**, **AMBER** or **GREEN** depending on how much overall potential you feel each idea has.

Remember the simple goal here is to Do ONE thing really well for ONE specific client.

WHICH IDEA DO I CHOOSE?	Earning Potential	Passion	Confidence to Deliver	Time Freedom	Total
What I'm currently doing	4	7	10	3	24

WHICH NICHE DO I CHOOSE?	Can they afford me?	Passion - Do I like working with them?	Confidence to Deliver the result	Total
Training comms teams	10	5	1	16

STEP 5 Create Predictable Sales Via the 6-Step Sales Formula

How many of you go to a sales meeting or have a sales conversation, and don't do it with any real set plan or structure?

Essentially you are winging it!

Better still I often hear things like, "Put me in a room with my ideal client, and I can close 80-90% of the time!" The reality is often different, and now you have a better offer, which is more expensive.

I doubt you can keep a 90% close rate if you've doubled your prices.

Essentially you have a good conversion rate because, up until reading The Fearless Business Blueprint, you've been too cheap. Now, you've got to learn to sell.

We do this thing, when we meet someone at a networking event, and say, "That sounds interesting, would you like to go and meet for coffee?"

You go to the coffee meeting, and there's a bit of chit-chat, but you come out of it thinking, "Well, what was the point in that meeting?"

You can lose a sale from the very start of the meeting. Often, there's one thing missing. You forgot to set the agenda for that meeting with your prospect. I tend to be direct and lead the interaction from the outset.

When somebody invites me for coffee, I will ask them a simple question, "I'd love to meet up, but I don't tend to do coffee meetings because my time's valuable, and your time is valuable as well." followed by, "Are we meeting up for coffee so that I can run through my coaching programmes with you, or are you going to be selling your products to me? I'm happy either way but I'd like to be clear on the agenda now." You give them the option of what the agenda is going to be during the initial meeting.

Having a Framework Means You Don't Miss Steps Out!

When you meet up for coffee and begin your sales process, you need to have a step-by-step plan that you stick to for each meeting. The reason why you've got to stick to this same step-by-step process with every prospect is so that, if at any point somebody says no, or they start to seem confused, you've got a framework which you can refer to.

You can test and measure it, and see if you missed out a step. For example, if you missed step number three, that's probably why your prospect didn't understand everything about the product or service you are offering. You can make a mental note to ensure you include step three during the next sales meeting.

The Customer Journey

I'm going to show you how to create predictable sales using my signature 6-Step Sales Formula. I'll share with you 6 simple steps which, if you introduce them into your sales process (if you have one), will absolutely transform your ability to sell.

STEP #1: Global Agenda - The Meeting Outline

The moment you sit down with a prospect, and you've gone through that initial small talk, "Hello, how are you doing? How's your family? What have you been up to this week?" The first thing you need to do is set a global agenda for the whole meeting. Lead with something like, "I just wanted to double check, before we get started, that we're here to chat about my coaching programmes and whether they are a good fit for you?"

Hopefully you'll receive a positive response. I have had meetings where we are at completely crossed wires so it's worthwhile checking the agenda at the start of the meeting.

Now if it's a strong, "Yes!", then that's a strong buying signal because you both know exactly why you're sitting the meeting. Your prospect is also "warm" - they are signalling that they are interested in your offer.

If they say, "No, that's not why I'm here!" you can set them straight on the agenda or even choose to adjourn the meeting.

That's it! Step 1 is complete and the Global Agenda is set.

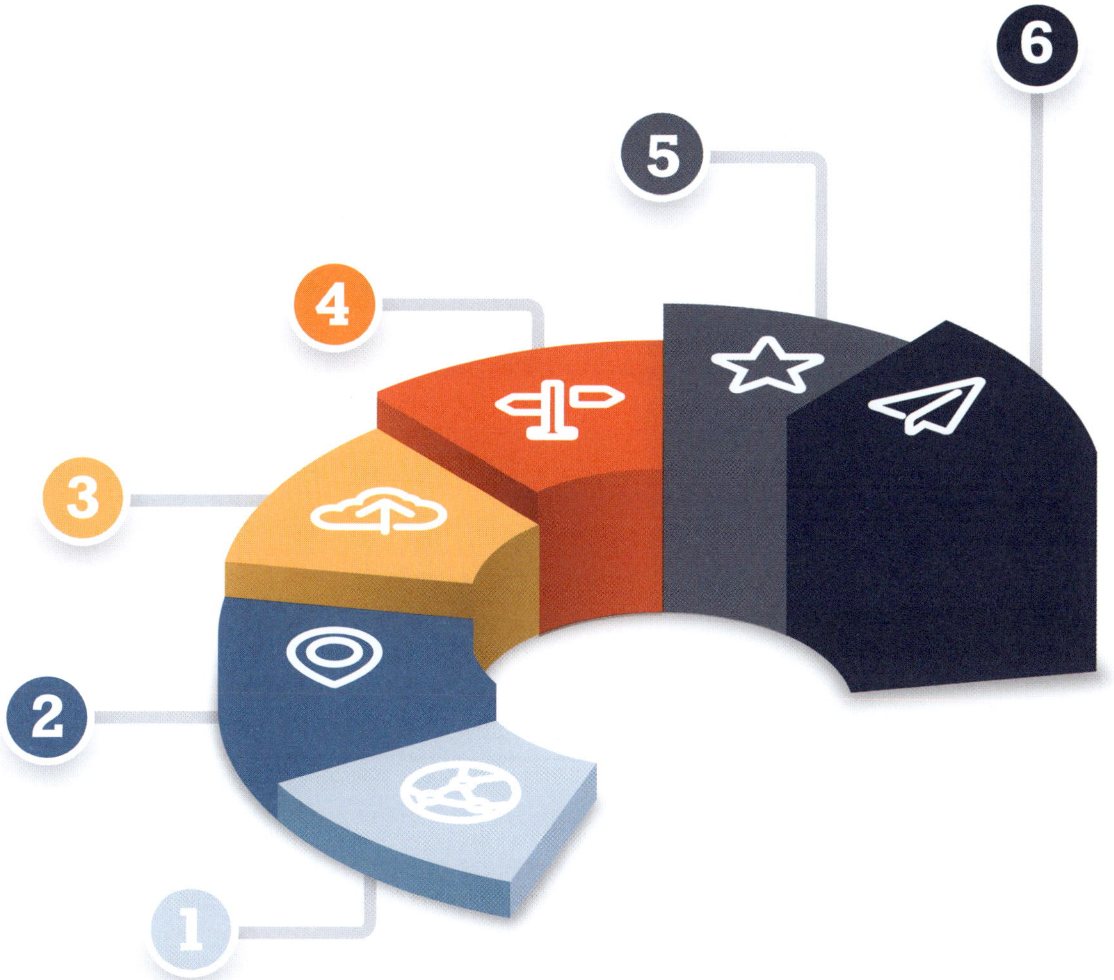

STEP #2: The Specific Agenda - Why Are We Here?

Next, you want to ask your prospect, "Is there anything specific which you would like to know, understand or ask me about in the next 30-minutes?"

The reason why the time scale is necessary is so that they know this is not just an endless coffee meeting, it has a purpose and a specific outcome.

There may be specific problems that your prospect has got within their business; there may be a question they want answering right now. Give your prospect the opportunity to ask specific questions about the outcome of the meeting.

I often ask, "Is there anything specific you wanted to get out of this meeting?"

Don't let them stop offering Specific Agenda Items. Typically, a prospect will rattle off two or three agenda items that they wanted to discuss with you during the sales meeting. When they pause (count to eight in your head - see my note about STFU), ask them, "Is there anything else?"

And they may offer one or two more Specific Agenda Items. Keep asking, "Is there anything else?" until they respond with, "No, I think that's everything!"

You are now building up a detailed brief around their doubts, or things that your prospect doesn't understand about your offer.

Take notes using a sharpie or a felt tip pen, writing out their prospects' Specific Agenda Items as they go. Write down your notes in front of them, so that they can see your notes. The reason you do this is to demonstrate to them that you're acknowledging what they're saying, and they know that you're creating an agenda as the meeting develops.

The list of Specific Agenda Items is now going to become the Script for your Pitch!

Read the list of items back to them and ask, "So, if I cover off all of the items you've mentioned you would feel confident in making a decision about investing in [insert your offer here]?"

STEP #3: Fact Find - We Do X Not Y

Once you've got their Specific Agenda Items noted, you can ask, "So, what do you know about me and my products or my business?" This is to get an understanding of what they know about you; they may have pre-conceived ideas. These ideas may be incorrect and now is your opportunity to correct your prospect.

Shifting from the web industry into business coaching meant I had to change people's perceptions around what I did. Being able to explain to my prospects what it is that I was doing was vital.

The way you frame this is, *"We do X, not Y."*

You might say something along the lines of, "Yes, I'm a brand consultant and designer, but I'm not an implementer, so I don't build websites." Reaffirming what it is that you do to the prospect so that there is absolutely no doubt about why they are attending the meeting and how you can help them.

I don't know if you've noticed, but you will barely speak during the first three steps. It is all about listening intently to your prospect. You haven't pitched. You haven't told them how much your products cost. You haven't said what the features and benefits of your products are. Make your sales meeting all about your prospect. It acts as an icebreaker. It makes them comfortable, feel at ease, and they feel heard. And I re-iterate, make sure you have written everything, they have said, down in your notes.

STEP #4: Feel Find - Where is Your Business Right Now?

The purpose of the Feel Find is to get an understanding of where their business head is at that particular moment in time.

Ask your prospect, "What challenges are you facing at the time within your business?" or "Why is this creating a problem within your business? What are your expectations were we to deliver a service or product to you? What are you hoping to get out of it?"

Delve deeper into the problems, pain points and challenges they are facing and get a feeling for the positive or negative experiences they are having in their business, right now.

Repeat the question, "Is there anything else?" Keep on probing and finding out information. Probing like this pushes your prospect into an emotional state where they can express their feelings while they process any information you feed them.

90% of a buying decision is based on emotions.

Emotions don't happen in a cognitive state. Feelings occur in our body. So, it's vital to get your prospect into this feeling space because 90% of their buying decision around your offer is based on how they are feeling.

Emotions help to determine whether they trust you, know you, and like you. The more you push them in that emotional space, the better chance we've got of getting an understanding of exactly what their needs are.

The final 10% of the buying decision is cognitive.

It happens after the buying decision is made, and is experienced as either buyer's remorse or consumer satisfaction. The person knows that they've made the right decision in buying your product.

Now you and your prospect both know exactly why you organised the meeting.

STEP #5: The Pitch - Your Time to Shine

Finally, it's your opportunity to tell your prospect about your offer. You can deliver your pitch in any way that you choose - although we teach clients a framework called the 3 Core Pillar Offer which I will link to in the action steps if you need something more concrete.

Refer back to the Specific Agenda Items and everything you uncovered during the Feel Find, and say, "Yes, I can fix that problem, and this is how/why."

Deliver value at all times. Demonstrate the outcomes and results your offer will give your prospect.

Tell your prospect about the guaranteed outcomes and deliverables that your product or service offers. DO NOT tell your prospect the price. I would recommend delivering a moment of silence (count to eight in your head) and wait to see what their reaction is.

Your prospect will likely respond with, "So how much does it cost? When can we start? What are the next steps?" They will have further questions about your products or services.

There are three things that people are going to reject your pitch on:

Price... Product... or Person (i.e. You!)

I'll deal with the latter first because it's rare for someone to say, "I don't like you, so I'm not going to buy your product or service." If somebody says, "Oh gosh, that seems expensive." it's rare that if you demonstrate enough value that your prospect couldn't find that money from somewhere to pay for your products. If your product fixes a big enough pain point for them, they will find the money.

It's more than likely you haven't articulated all of the benefits, outcomes and results your product or service delivers.

You could throw the question back to them and say, "Well hey, is there something that I haven't explained? Or, "Have I missed explaining about my product? Do you need more information on the product to understand the value and why it's priced as it is?"

In the past I've asked prospects directly, "Well look, I know you can afford this. I know you understand the product and you can see that it will solve your problem, so is it me?"

If you're oversubscribed and busy, you can be that blunt with people, and rarely will they reply, "Well, no, Robin, I don't like you." Just be mindful that once you've done your pitch, the responses you immediately hear back are the 'buying signals'. If you carry on talking, you will never hear the buying signal from your prospect.

STEP #6: Next Steps - Close Like a Pro

Don't forget to close. If your prospect asks, "What happens next?" You can throw the question right back to them and say, "What would you like to happen next?" They might say, "Can you send me the contract? Can you send me your terms of business and just confirm your prices to me in an email?" And you say, "Yep, great, I'll get my assistant to send that over to you later on today."

Ensure you have one or two clearly laid out next steps for you and your prospect to undertake, "Great! Next up I will issue an invoice for the deposit and send over the coaching agreement. Will you be able to get both of those signed and returned to me within the next 72 hours?"

WARNING: You Can Still Lose the Sale, Even If they Say, "Yes!"

The trick to not losing a sale once you've got the acceptance and agreed the next steps, is to say as little as possible.

In the excitement of the purchase, your prospect might ask you what you've got planned for the weekend? If you start rattling on about the crazy party you're going to that involves champagne and lots of celebratory dancing; the likelihood is you will lose the sale.

You can still lose the sale because somebody might like you now, but they might not like you based on what you talk about and do in your spare time.

Once you've completed your pitch and closed it, keep your conversation minimal and just throw it back over to your prospect, "Just a quiet one for me. How about you?" That's a neat way of closing the meeting down in an understated way.

ACTION STEPS

1. Remember the Sequence If you fail to plan you are planning to fail, so be clear on the 6-Steps Sales Formula and don't deviate, skip steps or go backwards in the sequence or face losing your prospect.

2. Take Copious Notes - During the conversation and especially during the Specific Agenda make sure to write ALL of the agenda items down. This forms the basis of your pitch.

3. STFU - Moments of silence are important during the call to give your prospect time to think and also prevents you from losing the sale once the call is complete.

FURTHER STUDY: Scan the QR Code to download the template and watch the video for the 3 Core Pillar Offer framework

Many struggle to articulate their value and end sales conversations with the prospect feeling confused. It's especially important to nail The Pitch so your prospect feels you have a step-by-step process to deliver predictable results.

STEP 6 Implement Rocket Fuel Marketing to Help Clients Find You

I've been in business for 20 years, starting my first marketing agency in 2004. By 2016, I sold the agency and began mentoring other agency owners. This led to the forming of my coaching practice, Fearless Business, in 2017.

Initially, I followed traditional marketing methods, but I realised there are more impactful ways to generate leads en masse.

In fact, about 18 months into my coaching journey a coach joined me in my offices in town (before I went fully virtual) for an initial consultation, and I still remember a question she asked me vividly, "Robin, I think I'm a better coach than you are but I don't understand why you're so much more successful than me!"

I was a bit shocked at the question, but replied, "I'm curious, how many consultations have you booked recently?"

She slowly counted on one hand, "1, 2, 3…4, 5, 4, maybe 4 or 5."

"That's great!" I replied, "4 or 5 consultations in the last week, you should be doing fine?"

She looked puzzled, "No…in the last year!"

This is her's, and many small business owner's, biggest problem. Lack of action. I then listed off everything I had done in my first year in business:

48 speaking engagements

36 podcast guest appearances

2-3 networking meetings a week

I started my own networking event (as I couldn't get booked to speak, I started my own event and booked myself as the keynote…but that's a story for another day) anyway it became a thing and we had 600 guests over a dozen subsequent events.

I booked the Aerospace Museum down at Filton, Bristol and held a 250+ person event under the wing of a Concorde…twice!

And..most importantly…sat 125 consultations.This resulted in 44 clients signing up and £89k - the only year I've NOT done 6-figures in revenue.

Continuing at this velocity in 2018 I became fully booked…and burned out.

Mostly because I was driving halfway around the country every week for consultations, speaking gigs and client sessions.

In late 2018 my coach suggested I went fully online and stopped wasting 20 hours a week driving everywhere. It worked. I launched the first online Fearless Business Accelerator on 1st January 2019. Sold out all 30 spaces and had my first 5-figure launch, grossing £31,968 in revenue (I sold 2 extra spots after we launched).

…And then filled up those extra 20 hours a week with marketing activities.

Doing all the things the "gooroos" and experts tell you to do: social media; repurposing content; blog articles; short and long form video; email marketing; asking for referrals; launching a podcast; guesting on dozens of other podcasts; you name it.

…And, I burned out a second time.

Finally, at the end of 2022 I became anti-social!

Spending 25-30 hours a week doing social media and marketing when all I wanted to do was coach people was so demoralising. The only solution I found was to quit social media and reclaim that time.

I needed clients though, so what do you do instead?

STEP #1 - The Power of Intentionality

In 2023, I decided to focus on partnerships. I wrote a list of 10 people I wanted to partner with and made sure to show up in their world.

This is the first step: be intentional. Identify who you want to partner with and make a plan to engage with them. Make sure they align with your values. You likely already follow their content online and attend their events.

Ensure they have audiences of 100k+ or even 1m+ followers or subscribers. These 10 people will be your future partners.

Bonus Tip: On Instagram, X and LinkedIn you can follow your partner and then switch on the bell notification. This means that whenever they post something, a notification appears in your feed. Be the first to like, comment and share their content.

STEP #2 - Show Up in Their World

The second step is to show up. Attend their events, support them, and make your presence known. For example, I paid extra for a VIP ticket to meet Steven Bartlett, founder of Diary of a CEO.

This allowed me to have a meaningful interaction with him before his talk (I was first in line, with a copy of Take Your Shot in Hand) and had a pic taken with him

STEP #3 - Add Value and Be Helpful

The third step is to add value. Don't just be a passive participant; be helpful. At an event with Chris Do, I provided a mic when they needed one.

This small act led to Chris acknowledging me in front of 150 people and even mentioning my book. Then later Chris invited me to help facilitate a workshop in Dubai and so I thanked him for paying for my conference ticket by hiring a yacht for the evening. Imagine getting 3 hours on a boat with someone like Chris Do, his sons and 7 other amazing entrepreneurs for less than the price of an expensive meal!

STEP #4 - Find Your Inside Man or Woman

The fourth step is to find your inside man or woman. Get to know the team members of the person you want to partner with.

Your partner is a busy person and may get too busy to answer your messages in detail. Take time to get to know their team and help them instead.

Like when I reminded one of Simon Squibb's team about doing a Book Review Campaign post book launch to keep it in the charts longer (me and him in the picture on the last page).

Another time, I helped some of Ali Abdaal's team members with coaching, which kept my name in their conversations.

STEP #5 - Offer the Silver Platter

The final step is to offer the silver platter. This comes in many guises:

Add Enormous Value: Bring value to your potential partners by connecting them with other influential people. For instance, I could introduce Chris Do to Ali Abdaal, benefiting both of them and strengthening my relationship with each.

Pay to Play: Many influential people run various memberships, masterminds and subscriptions. Don't think twice about signing up to these and supporting your potential partner. For example, I joined Daniel Priestley's *Key Person of Influence* programme over ten years ago and also license some of the KPI intellectual property, I now consider Dan to be a close friend and mentor:

Win the Game: When I wanted to build a partnership with Simon Squibb, he had not long launched HelpBnk.com. I thought, "What better way to get Simon's attention than to top the HelpBnk leaderboard!" I put in hours of work during June-August 2023…and, not only topped the leaderboard, but also won a $5,000 prize to boot. I've since given the money away to others who have helped and supported me on my journey.

Timeframes Don't Matter When You Run a Fearless Business

The five-step partnership framework is a powerful tool for generating leads. Be intentional, show up, add value, find your inside man or woman, and offer something valuable. This approach not only builds meaningful relationships but also drives massive lead generation.

The Results: Generating 3,000 Leads

By following these steps, I was able to generate 3,000 leads from a single podcast interview with Ali Abdaal. I offered a signed copy of my book, 'Take Your Shot,' as a gift to his listeners, which added significant value. This strategy turned a two-and-a-half-hour interview into a lead generation machine, equivalent to four years of traditional marketing.

The THREE best things about partnerships

It took me four and a half years to generate 3,000 leads the 'old way' using social media and just a train ride down to London and a chat with a friend to do the same in just two and a half HOURS!

Where the 'old way' of social media used to take up 25-30 hours a week (I even hired someone full-time for a year doing social media, it cost me £24,000 and I didn't get a single client!) and I spend maybe just 2-3 hours per WEEK nurturing my partnerships.

They are super fun, the people are fun, trips to Dubai are fun, having more leads than your business can cope with is great fun (kind of!), the events you get to go to are fun.

Fun, fun, FUN! Did I say Partnerships are *FUN*?!

The ONE downside of partnerships

They take a really long time to develop, I am talking months to years. And there's a small chance they may not lead to anything productive.

This is the crux of it. Most small business owners are so caught up in 'short-term thinking' needing to pay their mortgage and rent, they struggle to build the patience and resilience for building these long-term partnerships.

I, however, am stubborn, doggedly determined and long in the tooth. I would put off lots of £5k mini-rewards to land one big £250k win. Like Mel Gibson in Braveheart, "*HOOOOOLLLLLLDDDDDDDDD*!" and then make the ask when the opportunity arises whether it takes a year, two years or five years.

The Infinite Game

Simon Sinek talks about the purpose of business being the Infinite Game in his book.

Business is not the result of lots of short-term wins or losses. The Goal of business is to stay in business for as long as possible. Therefore, it is not a matter of IF my partnerships will land, it's a matter of WHEN.

The Ask!

Getting the ask right is the key final step in ensuring you maximise the opportunity from your partnerships. This means you need to consider:

When: Getting the timing of the ask right is imperative. Too soon you could appear over eager and too late and you've missed the opportunity.

What: If you ask too much, it will make it easy for your partner to say, "No!". Too little of an ask and you might miss out on maximising the opportunity. Or asking for the wrong thing, could end in disappointment also.

Who: If you ask the wrong person, you might miss out on the opportunity altogether. So make sure you ask the right person.

How: Simply asking for what you want isn't enough, the manner in which you make the ask is important, ask from a place of abundance and offer something in return.

Don't Ask: Believe it or not the best opportunities have arrived when I've overdelivered on value and the person has simply asked me, "Is there anything I can do for you, Robin?!" My answer is simple, "Thank you! Funny you should ask…!"

ACTION STEPS

1. Stop doing social media marketing! Especially if it's taking up too much of your time and not yielding substantial output and impact.

2. Be Intentional - Make a list of 10 prospective partners who you would love to hang out with who already have large audiences

3. Show up regularly and often in their world, adding value, being helpful, getting to know their team and give without take! TIME YOUR ASK!!

FURTHER STUDY: In the case study I share how I landed a partnership which resulted in 3,000 leads for my business and over £250k in revenue. **Scan the QR code to hear how Robin landed the podcast with Ali Abdaal.**

youtube.com/watch?v=hdsm3b52lb8

At the end of the day, if you don't ask you don't get, but equally you can over-egg your ask and not get anything at all. We have 8 sliding-doors moments in our careers as entrepreneurs, so you want to make the most of the opportunities when they come up.

STEP 7

Leverage: Build a Fearless Product

The traditional way of bringing an idea to market has always been:

However there is something interesting which is happening now in this digital, global marketplace where you can do things in a different order:

In the example you'll see that the money comes far sooner, and if you iterate and improve the idea earlier in the process and shift to sales and then design and delivery there is a far greater opportunity available.

Perry Marshall and Robert Schrobb break it down very neatly in their book, Detox, Declutter and Dominate, where they introduce the concept of the "Espresso Machine" product.

Marshall calls this "the principle of the $2,700 espresso machine." 80/20 says that for every 1,000 people who spend $5 on a latte, one will buy a gleaming stainless-steel espresso machine.

Notice I didn't say, "For every 1,000 people who buy a $5 latte, one will buy a $500 latte." Nobody is going to buy a $500 latte. But plenty of people will scratch their coffee itch with something far more expensive.

He goes on to explain that, "20% of your customers will spend 4 times the money to get something better."

No. of customers	Price	Web Design Business	Coaching Practice	Cyber Security Consultant	Total Income
1000	**FREE**	Website Audit	Business Diagnostic Workshop	Cyber-Risk Self-Assess-ment	**$0**
200	**$500**	One-Page Website	Breakthrough Session	Cyber Security Discovery Call	**$100,000**
50	**$2,000**	Brochure Style Website	Group Coaching Programme	CyberShield Essentials Programme	**$100,000**
10	**$10,000**	CMS Driven Website	1:2:1 Coaching	Fractional CISO (1:1 Advisory)	**$100,000**
2	**$40,000**	e-Commerce Website	1-Week Immersive Team Retreat	Red Team Immersion (On-Site)	**$80,000**

The challenge most people experience, and it comes from a very genuine place, is they want to perfect their products and services before taking it to market. This means designing the product in full, building the landing pages and funnel for it, carrying out a branding exercise and a quiz funnel, integrating it into their CRM, designing the brochure and getting several case studies all before launching the product.

The truth is, through being Fearless, you can sell an idea.

If you're clear on who the ideal customer is for your Fearless Product and the Dream Outcome it delivers, then get out there and start pitching your idea.

Iterate on your pitch - yes, the first 40 pitches will be rubbish, but you'll get better with practice - make you pitch slightly better each time by listening to feedback from your customer, and pitch again.

Eventually someone will say, "Yes! I need THAT!"
If you sell it for $40,000 you now have skin in the game and also 40,000 reasons to go and build out an absolutely stellar Fearless Product. Better still, your customer may even pay in full, in advance for the whole fee.

Which solves the second most common problem I see in business; Creating Positive Cashflow Cycles in your business.out on the opportunity altogether. So make sure you ask the right person.

ACTION STEPS

1. Come up with an idea for a Fearless Product which is 4x the price of your current, most expensive offer.

2. Now, get out there and pitch this offer to a minimum of 40 people. Improve your pitch each time, until someone says, "Heck yes! I need that!"

3. Now go and build out a killer solution for your customer, deliver the best experience and Dream Outcome that you possibly can do. Take payment up-front and in full.

FURTHER STUDY: One of my favourite books of all time is *Detox, Declutter and Dominate* by Perry Marshall and Robert Schrob.

Click on the QR code to the left to purchase your copy.

www.perrymarshall.com

You can be a busy fool making lots of low-ticket offers to prospects, or you can choose to move the needle hugely by offering high-ticket offers when the right customer. Don't get hung up on the details. What that pitch sounds like is, "I can sell you X, however I've got something far better for you, would you like me to tell you about Y?"

CASE STUDY

From Overworked and Confused to Trebling Their Turnover

Creative web design business, Anorak Cat, was founded by Richard and Amy to help other small businesses get online. From launch, Anorak Cat offered logo design where needed, website design, build and cost price hosting services. To attract customers via networking and online Facebook groups, they kept prices low (£400 per website), building up a portfolio of finished sites. That soon led to plenty of interest, however, their time and efforts weren't well rewarded.

The founders didn't have a clear strategy for growing the business; they quoted for each website and adapted their process every time.

Amy and Richard feared business would dry up if they charged more, even though Richard was working hard all the time. They knew he built professional Wordpress sites but felt they couldn't compete with larger web design agencies. Amy was going on maternity leave for the second time, making Anorak Cat the main source of income.

Fearless Business journey

After noticing Robin Waite's book, *Online Business Startup*, in the Local Business Network group, Richard ordered a copy to explore how it would help Anorak Cat. At the initial consultation with Robin, they re-visited their personal goals, defining what they wanted to achieve with Anorak Cat and their business strengths. After the free coaching experience, they signed up for regular coaching sessions, because they could see a huge opportunity to drive further changes with Robin's support.

"It's hard to explain the Robin effect; he's literally transformed our way of thinking, and subsequently our business. His knowledge, expertise and experience is undeniable and I'd recommend him 110% to any business owner. He has helped us with every aspect of our business and created time for us as a family again.

We now have the confidence to say no to potential clients that don't fit in with our goals for example clients asking for a 24/7 support service, or working on websites built on a CMS other than WordPress which is our specialism. Our monthly sessions give us the advice and confidence we need to keep moving our business forwards."

Amy Stevens, Service Director

Each coaching session focused on an area of business strategy, raising Richard and Amy's awareness of product architecture, pricing, sales confidence and operations. Robin used visual models to explain the concepts, which helped Richard and Amy see how they could transform the business to support their family with a steady income.

Regular coaching sessions gives them consistent support, yet makes them accountable for driving through the changes.

Impact of the coaching

The first change was to get Anorak Cat's pricing sorted, and introduce packages where they charged more, raising the minimum price of a website from £400 to £800.

Richard said, *"He gave us the confidence to increase our prices and charge what we're worth."*

By applying Robin's model for Goal Setting, Richard and Amy realised that logo design fell outside of the core process of launching professional websites. They immediately withdrew that service, saying, "No!" even to new startups who needed a logo for their new website. Full branding services were later reintroduced as they scaled into an agency model.

Robin helped Richard and Amy to review the lifetime value of their customer relationships.

Existing customers have a great experience with Anorak Cat, benefitting from proactive and ad hoc support from Richard as well as basic hosting.

When analysing the amount of follow up time, they realised they could adjust their services to achieve higher Customer Lifetime Value by keeping websites up to date and secure for their happy customers. This led to another product change: the launch of properly priced hosting and support packages, based on the size of the client's business and their website maintenance needs. Robin helped raise Anorak Cat's hosting fees from just £8/month to between £79-179/month depending on the clients' support requirements.

As great customer service sits at the heart of Anorak Cat's business, Robin has advised Richard and Amy in their subsequent coaching sessions on how to streamline their business processes.

The recommendation to create a Default Diary has improved their weekly time management. It enables them to spend more time focusing on looking after clients, developing the business and starting conversations with potential new clients. Anorak Cat now systematically tracks their job progress and sends every client a monthly website report.

"Robin makes a point of being available for us all the time to answer any questions or help us in between sessions. Having a coach has removed the anxiety from running our business, it's made it much more exciting and given us the motivation to push our

Richard Stevens, Managing Director

This summary outlines website performance and any maintenance work Richard has done. Where work exceeds the agreed time, Anorak Cat can easily charge for it separately or transfer the customer onto a more suitable support package.

In the seven months of working with Robin, Anorak Cat has doubled the number of clients they serve and trebled their monthly turnover. In addition to their coaching sessions, Amy and Richard have participated in Robin's '7 Day Fearless Pricing challenge.'

This intense business analysis exercise inspired Richard and Amy to revisit their potential income and pricing packages. Under Robin's guidance, Anorak Cat operates with consistent processes and delivers outstanding customer aftercare, creating a strong foundation for recurring revenue.

LAST WORD

How to Start Your Very Own Fearless Business

As an entrepreneur you will face challenges every single day. There's a chance that people outside of your inner circle will call you crazy.

Ignore them!

With 20+ years running small businesses I've started to see trends, not only in my own business but in clients' businesses also. They go through cycles. It is very predictable. Every 3 years they all roll through the 4 Stages of Business Growth.

In my agency we experienced the cycle 3 times, in my coaching business I've been through it twice already. And it will happen again.

In short, you want to purposefully break things in your business when you start to feel the Imposter creeping in, stay in the Fear Zone for as little time as possible and force the Breakthroughs to happen so you can spend as much time in Consolidation as you possibly can.

Why Break Your Business?

There is this thing called Survivorship Bias where only 5% of businesses get to celebrate their ten year anniversary.

By outlasting your competition there is no outcome other than for your business to be a success. People know, like and trust businesses that have been around for a long time. They assume you must know what you are doing and that you are doing things the right way. You have the reviews, the personal brand and the clients.

When your business is up against the wall it forces you to creatively innovate and solve your way out of problems. Zig when everyone else zags. It is scary though. Be prepared to do the things everyone else is too afraid to do.

During one dip into the Fear Zone we 5x'd our hosting fees in my agency just after the 2008 financial crisis hit. Everyone else was in a race to the bottom with their prices. We quintupled them. We lost 40% of our clients. 30 days later our Profit and Loss accounts showed a 2.5x increase in hosting fees. Our support calls dropped by 80%.The clients who didn't value our services left and took many of their problems with them.

Another time, my lead generation machine whirred into action, I was booking too many low-value calls, so I purposefully broke my funnel and switched it OFF! I instantly spotted the problem, innovated and fixed it. Doubling my conversion rate with half the calls. I could serve again at a far higher level than before.

There can only be one who is most expensive in the market, so why can't it be you?

Focus on gathering a tribe of high value clients, who love what you do and whom you can get amazing results for. Aim to earn double the income but with fewer higher paying clients.

Move away from the naysayers, the negative Nancies, your doubters and those who disagree with you.

Find other Fearless Business owners who are on the same mission. They will pull you through.

Support you. Innovate with you. Champion you.

Fear the things in business, ever-so-slightly less, so you can achieve your goals.

You can truly, once and for all, become the owner of a FEARLESS BUSINESS.

TAKE ACTION

Apply for a FREE Coaching Session with Robin

www.robinwaite.com/app